KT-483-263

WITHDRAWN
LIBRARY &
SERVICE

The Niger

illustrated by

Ron Stenberg

2100052227

E.L.R.S.

Macdonald
Educational

S026296

966.21E

The river Niger

The river Niger rises high in the mountains of Futa Jallon, just on the border between Sierra Leone and Guinea. As it flows down from the mountains, the Niger is joined by several tributaries, and gradually grows in power and size. Water at the source of the Niger takes nine months to flow the 4000 kilometres to the sea. High in the Guinea mountains, the river flows through thick forests. Near the town of Bamako, the Niger leaves the forest and enters a great plain which is flooded in autumn every year. There is not much rain here, and the floods come from heavy rains in the mountains. The floods are important for growing grain and rice, and also for fishing. During the dry season, livestock graze on the land which was flooded.

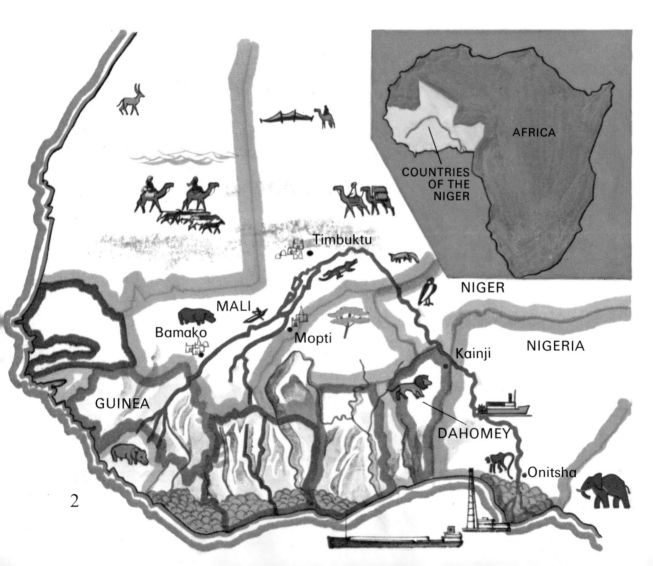

AFRICA

COUNTRIES OF THE NIGER

NIGER

Timbuktu

MALI

Bamako

Mopti

Kainji

NIGERIA

GUINEA

DAHOMEY

Onitsha

Near Timbuktu, the Niger leaves the flood area and flows for a long way through dry, almost desert country. From the town of Say onward, the river flows through an area where farming is easier because there is more rain. The Benue, the biggest of all the Niger's tributaries, joins the Niger at Lokoja. Hydro-electric plants are being developed where there are rapids. Further on, at Onitsha, the Niger starts to spread out to form a vast delta.

Long ago, large animals such as lions, giraffes and elephants, roamed in the country on either side of the Niger. Today, few of the big game animals remain, although there are still large numbers of crocodiles and hippopotami in the river.

The Tuareg

Many different tribes of people live along the Niger, each with their own language and way of life. In the area north of the great bend in the Niger, live an ancient Muslim tribe called the Tuareg. The Tuareg are nomads, who roam the Sahara desert looking for pasture and water for their flocks of goats, sheep and camels. They live in great low, black tents, which can be erected quickly at each new campsite.

The Tuareg are a proud and warlike people. Men almost always wear a veil which covers all of their faces except for their eyes. The Tuareg normally wear clothes dyed dark blue with indigo. The indigo also stains their skins, and this has given them the nickname of 'the blue people'. The men and boys tend the herds of animals, while the women and girls collect firewood, cook, spin wool, cure and dye leather, and look after the small children.

Until recent times, the Tuareg were vital to traders crossing the desert. They organised caravans, or supplied camels, or acted as guides. They also mined salt in the Sahara, and brought it to the south, where salt was very scarce.

Today, the traditional way of life of the Tuareg is threatened by change. Most of the goods from the Niger region are now transported by river and railway. Tuareg caravans are rarely needed.

The Tuareg, and other desert people, have also suffered the effects of terrible drought in the Sahara. More and more Tuareg have to give up their nomadic lives, and set up homes in towns and villages.

Tuaregs gather salt from salt pits. The water evaporates and the salt collects around the edge.

spinning

dyeing goatskin

5

The Sorko

A tribe called the Sorko live in the central flood plain through which the Niger flows, and along the great bend of the river through the desert. The Sorko have lived on the banks of the Niger since ancient times, and have always been renowned as skilled fishermen and boatmen.

In the flood season, the river rises and overflows its banks. Many Sorko villages are completely cut off by water, and the only way to travel is by canoe. Mosquitoes breed so fast and become so numerous, that the people dance all night long, as it is impossible for them to sleep. Dogs often sleep or rest under the water, leaving only their nostrils above the surface in order to breathe.

As well as fish, the Sorko find other kinds of food along the river Niger. Men search for crocodile eggs along the sandy banks. They look for a small heap of sand with marks of the mother crocodile's feet and tail. They may also see a ring of little insects crawling round it. The hunter feels for the eggs with his spear, and then digs them out by hand. There may be more than a hundred eggs in one nest. The eggs are taken home to be boiled or fried.

Hippopotami are hunted for their meat and their fat which has many uses for the Sorko.

The Nupe

the Etsu Nupe

Further down the Niger from the Sorko live another group of Muslim people called the Nupe, who live in the heart of modern Nigeria. The Nupe have been important and powerful for hundreds of years. They have traded with Hausa states to the north since about the 15th century. Some of the main exports used to be slaves and kola nuts, and a major import was horses. Today, Nupe exports include cotton, indigo, groundnuts and red peppers. The chief of the Nupe is called the Etsu Nupe. He has a colourful entourage of trumpeters and body-guards. The Nupe have their own language, but most children also learn to speak other languages such as Hausa and English.

The Nupe have a reputation for fine handicrafts, among which brass casting, ironwork, and glasswork are the most important. Brass is made from a mixture of copper and zinc, which is then melted down and poured into moulds. Iron is mined in Nupe itself. Nupe glass workers make beautiful jewellery and glass beads. They make their own glass, and also melt down old bottles to use for beads.

Nupe women do most of their cooking out of doors. These women are pounding maize to make meal.

Often water for cooking, washing and drinking has to be carried a long way from the well.

Most Nupe villages consist of clusters of conical huts like these. The huts are built of mud and straw, with thatched roofs.

The Ibo

The lower Niger is densely populated, except for the actual delta region, which is swampy. The largest single group of people in this area is the Ibo. The Ibo have never been united under one ruler, but instead are divided into small groups. The chief occupation of the Ibo is still farming, although many men have left the villages to search for work in the towns.

Ibo house

collecting palm fruit

In the past, farming methods and tools were simple and not very efficient. Recently, farming methods have been improved to provide food for the increasing population. The main traditional crops grown are yams, maize, cassava, plantain, cocoyam and pigeon pea. During this century several new crops such as rubber, cocoa, cashew nuts and coffee have been introduced and are grown on big plantations. The cultivation of these crops, mainly for export, has been encouraged by the government. In the swampy areas near the sea, rice farming is being developed.

A valuable oil is extracted by pressing the palm fruit.

stacking yams

Logs are cut into planks by the traditional pit-saw method.

Trees are also very important in the Ibo region, both as timber and for the crops they yield.

Many of the original trees have been cut down to make room for farming, and to be used as firewood. New trees are being planted to replace the old forests, and timber is an important industry.

Many trees are grown for their fruit. The main tree crops are bananas, plantains, oranges, grapefruit, pawpaw, avocado, mangoes, kola nuts, castor oil beans, and coconuts. Most valuable of all is the oil palm, from which palm oil is obtained and exported.

11

The Songhay empire

Along the northern bend of the Niger river a people called the Songhay built up a great empire. The Songhay empire rose to power very rapidly in the 15th century, largely under a conqueror and warrior called Sonni Ali. A city called Gao, on the banks of the Niger, became their capital. Gradually the influence of the Songhay spread out from Gao and other centres, until they controlled a huge area, including much of the desert in the north. All this territory was ruled by local viceroys and governors. The Songhay had a large army of both cavalry and infantrymen, as well as a navy on the river Niger.

At the beginning of the 16th century, a Songhay Muslim general seized the throne. His descendants, called the Askiyas, ruled the empire until 1591. This was the golden age of Timbuktu as a centre of Muslim learning and culture. There were many schools, and scholars studied and discussed large volumes written in the Arabic language and script.

Trade flourished in the great empire, and many merchants prospered. Wealthy merchants, scholars and members of the royal court were surrounded with luxury and riches. They ate from fine trays and bowls shaped in brass, which had been brought from Morocco, together with brocades for the men's robes. Rich wives had many servants to care for their children and home. They stained their nails and hair red with a plant dye called henna, and outlined their eyes with black antimony.

In the country, agriculture improved for many people. Canals were dug to provide irrigation, and the growth of trade gave farmers a reliable outlet for their goods. But not everyone benefited in the Songhay empire. Whole tribes were reduced to slave status, so that the Askiyas could sell their children in order to buy horses for the Askiyan armies.

12

13

Timbuktu

It was perhaps during the early part of the 12th century that the ancient city of Timbuktu grew up where the river Niger meets the Sahara desert. It became the meeting point for those travelling along the river, and those travelling over land. According to legend Timbuktu was named after an old slave woman who took care of travellers' possessions.

Today, the name Timbuktu represents somewhere exotic and mysterious. Travellers dream of going there, but many are disappointed when they see the city. Even during the 16th century when Timbuktu was at its most splendid, it was described as having no gardens and few trees. The houses were built of brown clay and the landscape was a monotonous expanse of sand and sky. It was the wealthy merchants and the travellers themselves who made Timbuktu exciting and colourful. Timbuktu became a centre of the Muslim religion in West Africa, and many people went there to study.

Moroccan conquest

About 1580, the Sultan of Morocco, Ahmad al-Mansur, began making preparations for the conquest of the Songhay empire, in the hope of gaining control of the gold fields beyond. He formed an army of 4000 of his best soldiers, made up of infantry musketeers and cavalry armed with muskets and lances.

The desert crossing was very hard, as the water supplies along the way were hardly enough for thousands of people with horses and camels. In 1591, when the Moroccans were close to Gao, the capital city, they were met by the Songhay army. The Songhay fought bravely but their arrows were of little use against the Moroccan guns.

The surviving Songhay warriors fled across the Niger in their boats, but resistance to the Moroccan forces continued. In Timbuktu, the Moroccans built boats, followed the Songhay and gained control of the land along the Niger bend. Large numbers of Songhay took to the forests and continued to resist the Moroccans.

Morocco never captured the gold fields which lay beyond Songhay. The government in Morocco found it impossible to control Songhay from across the desert. They lost interest in it, but the damage had already been done—the great historic empire of the Songhay was broken up and its strength destroyed.

Trade across the desert

Many centuries ago, the Sahara desert was not such a harsh barrier as it is today. The climate was more moist, and ancient rock paintings show that all kinds of animals, and even people, lived in areas which now are only rock and sand. Records show that as early as 500 B.C., there was travel across the Sahara. However, it was not until the first century A.D., after camels had been imported from Arabia, that large-scale travel and trading across the desert became common. Traders travelled in large groups, often with thousands of camels to carry food, water and trading goods. These groups were called caravans. The camel caravans used several different trading routes across the desert, and Timbuktu and Gao became very important trading centres. Many dangers and hardships faced the caravans on their journey.

The safety of the caravans depended on the skill of their guides. Guides had to lead the caravan safely from one waterpoint to another, or everyone would die of thirst. There were some guides who were blind, but could find their way just by the feel and smell of the land. Sandstorms and attacks from marauding tribesmen were some of the hazards faced by the travellers.

The most important articles exchanged across the Sahara were salt and gold. Gold was the main export from West Africa. Slaves were also an important export. In exchange, salt was brought into West Africa. Other imports were copper, horses, weapons and many kinds of luxury goods. Today, trans-Saharan trade has been greatly reduced. Most trade to and from West Africa now travels by sea, not across the desert.

Explorers

Mungo Park was born in 1771 at Foulshiels in Scotland. He was the son of a crofter.

Many European explorers led expeditions to the Niger river. Several lost their lives before the full course of the river was known. Among the first was a Scotsman called Mungo Park, who began his first expedition in 1795. He reached the Niger but had to turn back after being robbed of all his belongings. In 1805 he set off again with 38 Europeans. Of these, only seven survived to reach the Niger at Bamako. They sailed down the Niger in a canoe, but all were killed by hostile people at Bussa.

Other explorers tried to map the Niger.

In 1825, a naval lieutenant, Hugh Clapperton, arrived at the Niger with his young servant, Richard Lander. Clapperton died of fever at Sokoto, but Lander managed to get back to England. In 1830 Lander and his brother returned to the Niger at Bussa, and set off downstream by canoe. In Nupe country they were given a guide and a strong canoe. They continued down the river, and reached the delta. They were captured by Ibo warriors, but escaped and got back to England in 1831, having mapped the unknown lower course of the Niger.

Richard Lander left home at the age of 9. He was only 21 when he first arrived in Africa.

Slavery

Slavery existed along the Niger river, as in other parts of Africa, for many centuries. There were many slaves in the time of the Songhay empire, and even before this time people in the Niger region had practised slavery locally. There was also an active trade in large numbers of slaves across the Sahara desert, with the states to the north. A third form of slavery was the trans-Atlantic slave trade, which began when Europeans came to Africa. The first were the Portuguese, who discovered the sea route to the West African coast in the 15th century. The first shipment of slaves was taken to Portugal in 1441. After the discovery of the Americas, slaves were shipped across the Atlantic, to work on the plantations and farms, in the mines, and in their owners' homes. Ships from England, Spain, Holland, and elsewhere joined in the trade as demand for slaves grew. In the 18th century, the trans-Atlantic slave trade reached its peak.

Many slaves were taken northwards by Arab slave traders.

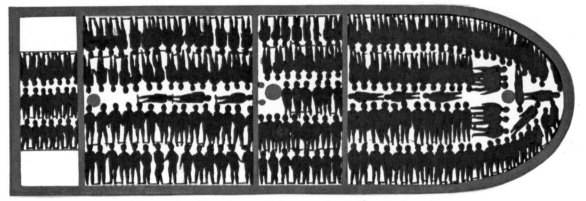

A 19th century diagram of a slave ship to show how the slaves were crowded in. Many slaves died during the journey.

Gradually, people in Europe turned against slavery and its cruelties. In 1807 Britain abolished the slave trade and tried to stamp it out. Sometimes, slave ships were stopped on the way to America, and the slaves were freed and returned to Africa.

By 1888, slavery was abolished by all countries in Europe and America. By this time there were many thousands of freed African slaves and their descendants in America and the West Indies. The trans-Saharan slave trade and local African slavery still continued for some time after this.

After the abolition of slavery, slave traders like these were arrested for illegal trafficking.

23

Christianity and missions

Samuel Adjai Crowther was born about the year 1806 in the town of Oshogun. When he was about fifteen, Muslim slave raiders destroyed Oshogun and captured Adjai, his mother and sisters. Adjai was sold several times, and passed from owner to owner. Then he was put on board a slave ship going to Brazil. The ship was captured by the British Navy who were then trying to put an end to the slave trade. With other freed slaves, Adjai was taken to Freetown, where he learnt to read and write. He was baptised and given the name Samuel in 1825.

Samuel continued his schooling in Freetown, and briefly in England. In 1843 he became a priest, and returned to West Africa as a missionary for the Church Missionary Society. He went with several expeditions up the river Niger, and wrote books about his travels.

In 1857 Samuel started a completely African branch of the Church Missionary Society, which was called the Niger Mission. Its main work was to set up Christian missions along the Niger river.

In 1864 Samuel Crowther became the first, black African, Anglican bishop. He was consecrated in Canterbury Cathedral in England.

Samuel Crowther carried on his work with the Niger Mission until he was over eighty years old. He translated the Bible into African languages, such as Yoruba, Nupe and Ibo.

Because of the work of Samuel Crowther, and other dedicated people, many churches and missions were built. As well as teaching religion, missions often set up schools and hospitals. Today there are many Christian churches along the lower Niger, and the area is one of the most strongly Christian in all Africa.

Colonial rule

A missionary on his rounds.

The first Europeans to become interested in West Africa were the Portuguese, who began by trading for gold, and later for slaves.

The expanding slave trade brought interest from other European nations. When slavery was abolished, people hoped that other trade would replace it. In the Niger delta, an important trade in palm oil developed. Palm oil was valuable as a lubricant for machinery in the growing industries of Europe. A strong feeling of competition grew between the great European powers, especially between France and England, who had often been rivals in the past. There was also religious concern for Africa.

African girls were taught domestic skills to become servants for Europeans.

During the last quarter of the 19th century, European powers gained control over most of West Africa. They wanted to enlarge their empires, and to control trade. Often there was also a wish to help Africa by ending slavery, by bringing, Christianity or by improving living standards. In some places the local people were content with European colonial rule, but others rebelled and fought. Colonial rule gave many benefits and wealth to Europe. It also brought improvements to Africa in transport, education, and medicine.

A polo match between British and Africans.

A meeting or 'palavar' between colonial officials and African chiefs.

But West Africa wanted to be free. The British and French started to withdraw in the late 1950s and today the West African countries rule themselves.

Health and medicine

Many of the rivers of the world are breeding grounds for a variety of diseases. One of the most serious of these is malaria, which causes high fever. Even today, it is thought to be the greatest single killer in the world.

When Europeans first came to West Africa, they suffered greatly from malaria, and other diseases.

So many people died on the West African coast that a song was made up about the bay at the western half of the Niger delta:

> "Beware and take care of the Bight of Benin,
> There's one comes out for forty goes in."

It was known that chinchona bark, from which the drug quinine is made, acted as a medicine against malaria. After some research it was found that quinine could also be taken to prevent malaria.

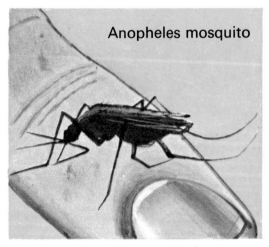

Anopheles mosquito

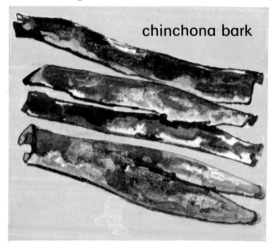

chinchona bark

Although a medicine was known, the cause of the disease was still a mystery. In Europe during the 18th century, people thought that mists and 'bad air' caused it. In the 19th century, a British doctor, Dr. Ronald Ross, discovered that malaria was carried by the female Anopheles mosquito.

Malaria is dangerous to Africans as well as to Europeans. Many children die of it. Those who survive have occasional attacks of malaria throughout their lives.

During this century, much has been done to reduce mosquitoes and control malaria. Standards of health and medicine are improving all the time along the Niger. Hospitals and clinics are being built, and people are being educated in better hygiene.

Boats on the Niger

The oldest and most common form of transport on the river Niger is the canoe. Canoes vary tremendously in size, shape and construction, depending on the area and for what they are used. Explorers often travelled along the Niger by canoe. A Frenchman, Caillie, travelled in a huge canoe, over 30 metres long with a crew of 50 slaves. There were also many smaller canoes. They were very important for carrying food and could be rowed or paddled, or punted with a long pole. Some canoes were dug out of a single tree trunk. During the 19th century, small paddle steamers were brought in to work on the Niger. Early this century, bigger steamers were built which could carry heavier cargoes. But steamers could only work in good flood seasons when the river was deep enough. Today, there are a variety of modern craft; motor barges, passenger launches, cattle ferries, and even old dug-out canoes with outboard motors.

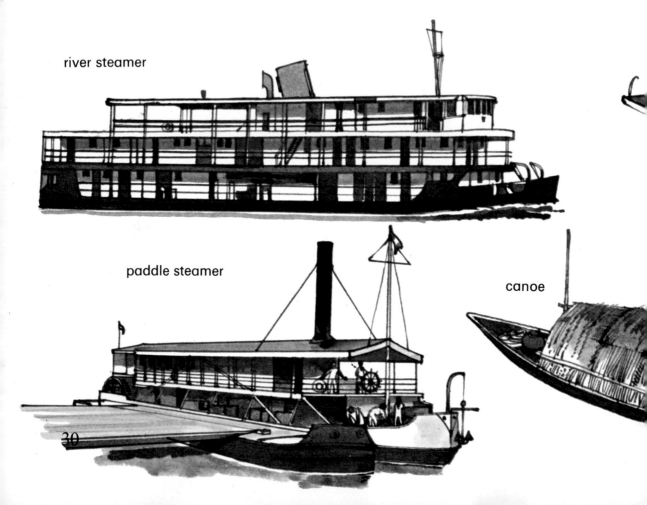

river steamer

paddle steamer

canoe

cargo ship

barge

punt

trading hulk

31

Crafts and craftsmen

Bronze is melted and poured into a mould. When it hardens, the bronze is engraved and decorated.

Basketry is one of the many Niger crafts which is both attractive and useful.

Gourds and calabashes are like pumpkins. Their shells are dried and then decorated.

Weaving is an important craft along the Niger. Cotton is woven into beautifully patterned cloth.

Potters usually work without a potter's wheel. They mould the clay with their hands.

Iron is found locally. Blacksmiths do fine wrought-iron work with simple tools.

Many houses along the Niger are decorated with mud sculpture or paintings.

There are many kinds of wood suitable for fine carving in the delta region of the Niger.

Traditional religions

Many people living in the Niger region, and in the rest of West Africa, are neither Christian nor Muslim, but instead have traditional beliefs which have existed for hundreds of years.

Religions may vary among different tribes, and in different regions. Often, people do not worship just one god like Christians or Muslims, but believe in a number of gods or spirits. Sometimes they believe that people who die become spirits, and have a power over the living, which may be good or evil. People may pray to the spirits of the dead, and offer sacrifices to them. This kind of belief is called ancestor worship.

Some people worship trees, rivers, the sun or the earth, or various kinds of animals. There are many ceremonies and festivals connected with different beliefs, which may involve dressing in special costumes or masks, feasting, dancing and making sacrifices or offerings.

Sorko dancers

One very important ceremony takes place every seven years at a place called Kaba, on the upper Niger. At these times, Kaba becomes the centre of a pilgrimage, and large numbers of people gather for the festival which lasts five days. A special hut, or shrine, is built and decorated. During the first night of the festival a story of the people's creation is told inside the shrine.

The story begins by God creating some seeds. Two characters called Faro and Pemba appear. Pemba wants to control creation, and when he fails, he steals some of the seeds. Later, his sister Mousso Koroni secretly plants the seeds. Faro comes down from heaven in the form of two fishes. The fishes chase Mousso Koroni, and when the Niger floods the fields, they eat the stolen seeds. Men come and reap the fields Mousso Koroni has sown. Faro is meant to be the power of good, and some say that he is himself the Niger.

A story of the Niger

Once, an evil spirit called Zin-kibaru lived in the Niger with his musicians. He had great power over the fishes and animals of the river.

One day a farmer called Faran was in his rice fields when he saw Zin-kibaru playing his guitar. All the fishes came from the river and ate Faran's rice.

Enraged, Faran went to fight Zin-kibaru. They met on an island and agreed that if Faran won he would take the Zin's guitar. But if the Zin won, he would take Faran's canoe.

Just as Faran started to win, Zin-kibaru muttered this magic spell: "The palm leaf despises the hippo!" Faran fell to the ground, and lost his canoe.

Faran went home ashamed and sad, but his mother said he was stupid. She told him he had to fight the spirit's spell with another spell. She taught him a good one to use.

So Faran went to fight Zin-kibaru again. As the spirit cast his spell, Faran replied "If the sun strikes it, what happens to the palm leaf?" The Zin fell down.

Seeing that Faran had conquered Zin-kibaru, all the musicians jumped into the river Niger, and left their musical instruments behind on the bank.

Faran seized the guitar, Zin-kibaru's harpoon, and all his slaves, and took them home in triumph. He had conquered the power of the river spirit.

Modern countries of the Niger

NIGERIA

DAHOMEY

NIGER

MALI

GUINEA

The boundaries of the modern African countries through which the Niger flows did not exist before the 19th century. The modern boundaries were set up by authorities. Often, frontiers did not match any very important local divisions. But the new frontiers remained even after the Europeans left, and the countries became self-governing.

As people took more interest in developing their new nations, old tribal loyalties gradually became less important. Now the independent African countries have existed for many years.

The Niger flows through five countries: Guinea, Mali, Niger, Dahomey, and Nigeria. In the 1960s in Nigeria, people in the eastern area around the lower Niger river rebelled against the central government. They tried to form a state of their own, called Biafra. This caused a civil war in Nigeria in which Biafra was defeated.

The Niger rises in the mountains which lie just on the border between Sierra Leone and Guinea. From the Guinea highlands, the Niger descends into Mali through which it flows for a great distance. It was within the borders of modern Mali that the ancient empires of Mali and Songhay rose and fell. The famous cities of Timbuktu and Gao are also in Mali. Beyond Gao, the river swings southwards and crosses into the country with its own name; Niger. For about 160 kilometres the river itself forms the border between Niger and Dahomey to the south.

Then the river enters Nigeria, through which it flows until it reaches the sea. Of all the countries through which the Niger passes, Nigeria is by far the biggest. The population is about 55 million, which is five times as great as the populations of Guinea, Mali, Niger and Dahomey all put together.

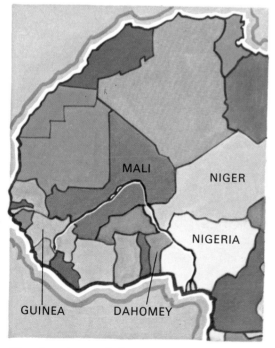

The borders of the countries of West Africa showing the Niger river.

New roads are helping to improve communications in West Africa.

The Niger today

In 1968 the Kainji Dam was completed on the Niger river. The dam created a huge lake behind it, which covered the old town of Bussa. A new town has been built near the dam and is called New Bussa. Dams like this provide hydro-electricity for power. They also allow flood waters to be controlled, which improves irrigation and navigation.

During the past few years, improvements have been made to the transport and communication systems in West Africa. Bridges have been built across the Niger for both road and rail.

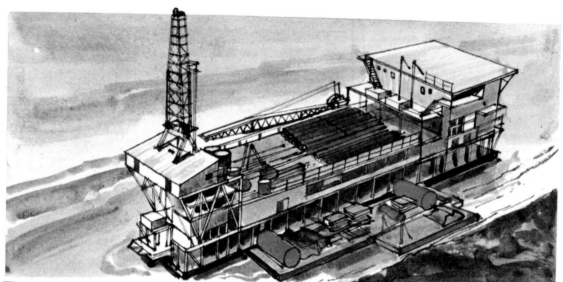

The first discoveries of oil were made in Nigeria about 25 years ago. Several large oil-fields have been found, both on land and off-shore in the Niger delta area. Drilling for oil is made difficult by the swamps, but Nigeria is now one of the Commonwealth's top oil-producing countries. Most of the oil is exported and provides about 90 per cent of Nigeria's foreign earnings.

Until recently, agriculture in West Africa was on a simple scale, but farming methods are being improved. Production of crops has greatly increased with the use of modern machinery and fertilisers.

Foods from the Niger

Many exotic fruits and vegetables are grown in the Niger region of West Africa.

Yams are a root crop which are very nutritious, but difficult to grow. They are cooked in much the same way as potatoes.

Cassava is another root vegetable. It is easier to grow than yams, but lower in food value. Cassava is usually pounded before being cooked.

Plantains look like large bananas, but they are bitter and coarse. They are usually fried and eaten as a vegetable.

Maize can be eaten boiled or roasted on the cob, but is more often made into a thick gruel or porridge.

Pawpaws and mangoes are both fruits, which are generally eaten fresh. Pawpaws are a kind of melon. Mangoes have the texture and colour of peaches. They are sometimes used in making chutney, and are also tinned for export.

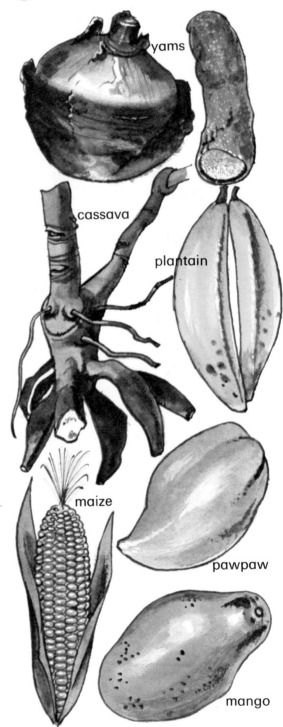

yams

cassava

plantain

maize

pawpaw

mango

Poem from the Niger

There is a Fulani poem from the upper Niger, about an argument
between the water and a palm tree. They are arguing about which is
more important; water or palm trees. This is part of it:

The Water and the Palm Tree

Water: If there were no water,
then there would be no more life,
No more butter to be churned,
No more posts on the fire,
No more sprouting in the fields or in the bush,
No more camps or cities,
No more parents, and so no more children!

Palm tree: The matting on the roof, the fan,
Everything that is plaited in our islands,
All that, thanks to our palm trees—
Even the fish basket,
All that, thanks to our palm trees.

Water: Take these palm trees away from me;
Get up, leave room for the flood!
Flood, rise, Mother of lives!
Water the cattle and sheep,
Flood, rise, Mother of lives!

Palm tree: If the crocodile is there,
We shall see you bolt pretty quickly!

Index